Landmark
BOOKS

Clara Barton

FOUNDER OF THE AMERICAN RED CROSS

CLARA BARTON

FOUNDER OF THE
AMERICAN RED CROSS

———— ★ ————

by HELEN DORE BOYLSTON

Illustrated by PAULA HUTCHISON

RANDOM HOUSE · NEW YORK

Sixth Printing

Copyright 1955 by Helen Dore Boylston
All rights reserved under International and
Pan-American Copyright Conventions
Published in New York by Random House, Inc.,
and simultaneously in Toronto, Canada, by
Random House of Canada, Limited
Library of Congress Catalog Card Number: 55-5824
Manufactured in the United States of America

Gratefully to Helen H. Robinson

Contents

Clara Barton

FOUNDER OF THE AMERICAN RED CROSS

1

Six Fathers and Mothers

The large, thickly frosted cake stood on a low table in the farmhouse living room. Beside it stood three-year-old Clara Barton, a tiny dark-haired girl in a red dress and red shoes and stockings. Her brown eyes were big with excitement and importance because she was to cut and serve the cake.

Her smiling family waited with plates in hand —her father and mother, her grown-up sister, Dorothy, her almost grown-up brothers, Stephen and David, and Sally, next youngest, but ten years older than Clara. The last member of the family, Clara's white dog, Button, beady-eyed and with agitated tail, waited confidently at the end of the line.

Button's confidence was not misplaced. When everyone else had been served, he received his piece, which vanished in one gulp. Clara was distressed.

"Why didn't he thank me?" she demanded seriously of her mother. "Everyone else did."

The family laughed and waited, knowing what was coming next.

Clara turned back to the cake to cut her own piece; and the happiness on the little face changed to surprise, bewilderment and disappointment. There was no cake left. She had forgotten to save any for herself.

The first time this had happened there had been an amused chorus of, "She can have mine!" Clara's mother, however, had not approved of this.

"No," she had said. "She must not take back what she has given. She must learn to stand by what she does." There was a horrified silence before Mrs. Barton had added, "But there's no reason why you shouldn't *share* with her."

Clara Barton certainly learned to stand by what she did, but she never learned not to give away all of whatever she had, as occasion required. And she was always surprised to find that she had left nothing for herself.

Her name, actually, was not Clara, but Clarissa—Clarissa Harlowe Barton—for an aunt who, so Clara was told, had been named for the heroine of a book popular at that time. The name seemed long and fussy to the little girl, and she began to call herself Clara as soon as she could talk.

She was born on Christmas Day, 1821, in her father's comfortable farmhouse in Oxford, Massachusetts. The farm was a very large one and the family, though hard-working, was always prosperous. The baby girl was regarded as a welcome Christmas gift by everybody.

She became the petted darling of her much older brothers and sisters, particularly her brother Stephen, until, as she said long afterward, she grew up with six fathers and mothers, all determined to teach her what each considered important. If life on the big farm could have been lonely without any children of her own age Clara had little time to find it out.

Her sister Dorothy, already a schoolteacher, taught Clara to read before the little girl was three. Stephen spoiled her and petted her, but he taught her arithmetic too. David taught her to ride almost before she could walk and, surprisingly enough, taught her carpentry. Sally, soon to be a teacher, helped with the book-work.

David taught her to ride almost before she could walk

When Clara was old enough, Mrs. Barton taught her sewing and housework. Captain Stephen Barton, whose great kindness of heart gave his youngest child her lifelong concern for the welfare of others, taught her military tactics—a strange subject for a little girl—but the one that Clara loved most.

Evening after evening the child sat in her father's lap before the open fire, listening to his stories of the days when he fought under General "Mad Anthony" Wayne.

She learned all about military rank. She learned about infantry, cavalry and artillery. She and her father arranged battles on the floor, using grains of corn for soldiers, and together they fought the war again.

"I want to be a soldier," she told her mother a dozen times a day. When her father came in at night, she would say, "Father, tell me again about the time you lay in the frozen swamp and drank water out of the horse's footprint."

It is not known exactly what Mrs. Barton thought of the petting, spoiling and peculiar instructions Clara received, but she once remarked to a friend that Clara had come out of it more level-headed than might have been expected.

Yet it was Clara's thorough understanding of military matters and conditions of war which was later to enable her to face a battlefield without surprise or shock. Her ability to ride any kind of horse saved her from capture.

There was, however, one thing about Clara which was a constant worry to her father and mother.

The little girl was an exceedingly timid child. She was afraid of cranky animals, thunderstorms, snakes, the dark, and especially people.

She was so terrified of strangers, even children, that she was hardly able to speak. When the time came for her to go to school, this became a real problem.

Perhaps, if she had been a little older, it would have been easier. She was not yet four years old when Stephen, carrying her on his shoulder through the snow drifts, took her to the little one-room school a mile from home and set her down in the midst of all the children. Clara was terrified, but the worried Stephen had to leave her there.

It was lucky for Clara that the teacher, Mr. Richard Stone, was young, kind and had children of his own. He was very gentle with the little girl, and finally persuaded her to sit down at one of the desks. When she seemed more relaxed, he asked her to name the letters of the alphabet. She named them in a voice that was barely more than a whisper.

"Can you spell cat?" Mr. Stone asked.

Clara stared at him numbly. Then a spark of pride came to her rescue. "I don't spell there," she said.

"Oh? Where do you spell?"

"I spell in artichoke."

She meant that she could spell words of three syllables, and artichoke was the first three-syllable word in the spelling book. Mr. Stone was startled, but he put her at once in the third-grade reading class.

Clara understood that he was pleased with her, and that helped. However, she remained too shy to make friends with the other children, was afraid to play with them, and if they laughed at her she burst into tears.

She was no better the next year when Mr. Stone left to start a private school of his own.

He was replaced by a very pretty young woman, Miss Susan Torrey. Clara adored her, but even Miss Torrey could do nothing to overcome Clara's shyness. Neither could her own sisters, Dorothy and Sally, when they taught her in the same school later on.

By the time Clara was eight years old and no less shy, her parents decided that something must be done.

"What *is* it?" Mrs. Barton asked her husband. "She's still scared to death in school—yet she'll let David toss her up on one of your wild colts, and she gallops everywhere without saddle or bridle, just hanging to the creature's mane. *That* would frighten most children out of their wits."

Captain Barton shook his head. "I don't know,

Sarah, what 'tis. Maybe we ought to send her to a boarding school—get her away from home and used to being with strangers."

There was such a school only a day's journey from home. It was Richard Stone's school, and he understood Clara if anyone could. Besides, she was very fond of him.

The matter was discussed for weeks, and arrangements were finally made with Mr. Stone. At last, one bleak April day, Clara Barton, aged eight, drove away with her father to a very different kind of life.

2

Tomboy

The new school was pleasant, the teachers kind, the other children friendly. Clara was wretched, not only from homesickness but from terror that she might do something wrong and be laughed at. She was still excellent in her studies, but this was of no help in overcoming her fears. She was even afraid to eat. At the long table in the school dining room, while the other children ate heartily, Clara refused nearly everything that was offered her. She became thin, pale and tired.

Mr. Stone, hoping to tempt her to eat, began to put food on her plate. Clara didn't touch it though she was ravenously hungry. One suspects that, whether Clara knew it or not, she was really on strike. And she won out, for ultimately her father had to come and take her home.

The family gave up. After that Clara was taught at home, sometimes by her sisters and brothers, sometimes by tutors hired to give her lessons in some special subject. She did not go to an outside school for some years.

Shortly after Clara's return home, a nephew of Captain Barton's died, leaving a wife and four children, two boys and two girls, between the ages of six and thirteen. Captain Barton bought his nephew's farm, which was near his own. His grown-up sons remained on the old place and ran it. He and Mrs. Barton took Clara with them to the new home, and invited the widow and her children to live with them.

This turned out well for everyone, particularly Clara, who, for the first time in her life, found herself part of a gang near her own age. Her four cousins were lively and afraid of nothing. They liked Clara and considered her one of themselves, including her in everything they did.

She had never played outdoor games before. Now she raced with the others, played hide-and-seek, jumped from the haymow, climbed trees, and scampered without thought over the narrow shaking log which served as a makeshift bridge over the little French River near by. She even rode the saw carriage at the neighboring mill, sitting on the great logs without fear.

She grew strong and muscular and came in at night with glowing cheeks and sparkling eyes. A great many of her terrors began to disappear, and to the astonishment of the family she asked to be allowed to go to dancing school.

Captain and Mrs. Barton would have been only too glad to send her. They had no objection to dancing. Unfortunately, their neighbors and the members of their church considered dancing sinful and an invention of the devil. The Bartons felt that they would be unwise to fly in the face of neighborhood opinion, and so, reluctantly, their answer to Clara was "no."

They did not dream how great her disappointment was, for she made no fuss about the refusal, accepting it without a murmur. But she cried herself to sleep more than one night, and she never forgot. Many years later, when Clara was fifty years old and in London, she hired a dancing teacher to come to her house and give her lessons. It is pleasant to know that she became a very good dancer.

Her next attempt to acquire a new skill had disastrous results.

Early one Sunday morning she was awakened by the boys—her cousins—throwing pebbles at

Soon the boys were going much too fast for a beginner

her window. If she would come out, they promised, they would teach her to skate. Nobody need know, for the entire household was asleep.

This would be breaking the Sabbath, which was forbidden by all their parents. Nevertheless, Clara went.

The boys fastened on her skates, tied a scarf around her waist, and, each holding an end, they started off, towing the delighted Clara. The ice, unhappily, was very rough, and the boys were going much too fast for a beginner. Clara tripped and fell, tearing one knee wide open and badly scraping the other.

None of the children had ever seen so much blood.

The frightened boys bound up Clara's knees with their none-too-clean woolen scarfs, and it was agreed that nobody would tell. But Clara must be careful not to limp!

She tried desperately to fulfill her part of the bargain, and the long skirts which girls wore in those days concealed the bulky bandages. That day, she managed somehow, but the next morning the wounds had stiffened and were agonizing. Poor Clara limped in spite of all her efforts, and Mrs. Barton began to ask questions. Clara admitted that she had fallen—she didn't say when or where—and offered the less injured knee for inspection. The other she kept concealed by her skirts.

Mrs. Barton was shocked by the condition of the "good" knee, soaked off the woolen scarf which was stuck to it, bathed the knee and dressed it. It is a pity that she didn't discover the state of the other knee, which was seriously cut and was already becoming infected from the scarf.

The result of this foolishness was exactly what might have been expected. Clara's knee and then her leg swelled hideously, became badly infected, and had to be operated upon. Clara was in bed for three weeks. During that time everyone was so good to her that she became more and more conscience-stricken. She brooded upon her disobedience to her parents until Mrs. Barton took pity on her, assuring her that she had not done the worst thing in the world.

"I disobeyed my father once," Mrs. Barton told her.

"What happened, Mother?"

"Well, Father had a beautiful, unbroken colt which I wanted very much to ride. Father forbade me to go near it."

"Then what?"

Mrs. Barton smiled. "I rode it anyway."

"Oh, Mother—you didn't!"

"Oh, yes I did!" Mrs. Barton paused maddeningly.

"What *happened*, Mother?"

"I got thrown."

Clara felt very much better.

3

Growing Up

Clara's normal happy life continued until 1832, when she was eleven years old. Then her brother David fell from a barn roof and was seriously injured. Clara had always loved him dearly—next best to Stephen—and she was frantic.

Mrs. Barton, thinking it would ease the child to do something for David, allowed her to help

23

around the sick room. To everyone's surprise, Clara turned out to be a born nurse. David clung to her, grown man though he was, for she seemed to understand by instinct what would make him the most comfortable. When she arranged his pillows they were always right. She knew when to talk and when to keep quiet. Her small hands were firm and gentle as she turned him. She was pleasantly cheerful but she never bustled.

Little by little she took over all his care—even to the leeches.

Leeches were the great cure-all in those days. They were a kind of blood-sucking worm which doctors used with the sick. People believed that "bleeding" a patient would help him, so they let the leeches suck his blood. Nowadays, when someone has a bad accident, the last thing anybody wants to do for the patient is to "bleed" him. He needs all his blood to regain his health and strength.

However, in Clara's day, the first thing done

for the patient was to bleed him, even if he had already lost a great deal of blood. People were bled for everything—headache, influenza, jitters, broken bones, fainting spells, or a state of depression.

There were a number of ways of doing this, but the most common and painless was to apply leeches here and there over the larger blood vessels. The leeches were black, slimy and unpleasant. When they had sucked all the blood they could hold, they fell off and were put back in their jar for use another time.

David was ill for two years. He was bled almost daily during that time, and it is a miracle that he recovered at all.

The doctor, finding the eleven-year-old child so capable, taught her to apply the leeches. Clara, who was terrified at the sight of a single drop of blood, was now confronted daily with a great deal of it. But it was all for David's good, and Clara was thinking of him instead of herself. She applied the leeches with great skill, and without knowing it, got used to blood and ceased to think about it one way or another.

It has never been explained why her parents allowed her to become David's sole nurse, staying with him day and night for two years, but she was, and she did. The only time she left him was when she went for a short ride on Billy, the beautiful horse given her by her father when she was ten years old.

David finally recovered, in spite of the continuous loss of blood. Clara, now thirteen and free to amuse herself like any girl in her teens, became increasingly gloomy. She grew pale, thin and listless. Though she tried to put up a cheerful front, she took very little interest in anything.

There was almost a year of this, which is a long time for anybody to remain in the dumps. Then a hired man of her father's fell sick with smallpox. Before anybody had time to interfere, Clara was nursing him. Her gloom vanished.

There was color in her cheeks again, her eyes were bright, her appetite was healthy.

Smallpox spread through the village, and Clara took on more patients. Of course, she caught smallpox, but she recovered rapidly and hurried back to nursing again.

If one wonders what Clara's parents could be thinking of to allow all this, it is easy to guess. They couldn't help themselves. The driving necessity of Clara's life was to be of service to others. She was too young to know this; she could only act as it drove her to do.

This need found its first release in service to a single human being—David. It drove her on, step by expanding step; to a handful of sick in the village; to a few hundred underprivileged children; to thousands of wounded men; and later to millions upon millions of the world's afflicted.

And nobody could stop her—not generals in the army, or governors of states, or even the

United States Congress, though they all tried at
one time or another, usually for reasons which
they sincerely believed to be good, reasonable
and wise.

So it is not surprising that Captain and Mrs.
Barton were unable to stop her nursing in the
smallpox epidemic, though their anxiety must
have been increased by the discovery that Clara
had stopped growing. She was five feet tall at
the age of fourteen, and she remained five feet
tall for the rest of her life—a tiny little woman
to swing the world by the tail.

4

Schoolteacher

David's illness and the smallpox epidemic had been anything but helpful in furthering Clara's general education. This did not please anybody, including Clara, who had liked to study, though she had not liked school. What was even worse, she was lonely for the first time. Her four lively cousins and their mother had moved away.

Stephen was married, and he and David were living at the other farm. Sally was married, too, and living on the other side of town. Dorothy was away teaching.

There were no children to romp with, no brothers or sisters to pet her and give her lessons. So at fifteen Clara went back to school again in North Oxford. She was still shy, but after her nursing experience school did not seem so alarming. She got along well enough and made top grades, as usual.

It was during this period that Clara overheard something which had an immediate effect on her life. She was at home recovering from mumps, of all things. Her father and mother were entertaining a guest, a Mr. Fowler, who was one of the leaders in the practice of phrenology. This was a study of the shape of the skull, with particular attention to any lumps or bulges on it. It was believed that these were caused by special developments in the brain, indicating character and tendencies, and pushing up the skull a little at that spot. The fact that the brain is soft, spongy, and tender, and the skull as hard as rock, was not taken into consideration. Yet phrenologists were often surprisingly accurate in their estimate of character.

Mr. Fowler was a good and honest gentleman who believed sincerely in phrenology. He had come over from England for a lecture tour, and at the time was staying with the Bartons.

Mrs. Barton asked his advice about Clara and her sensitiveness. Clara was lying on the couch in the next room and heard every word.

"She will always be sensitive," Mr. Fowler said, "and she will never assert herself—for herself; she will suffer wrong first. But for others she will be perfectly fearless. Throw responsibility upon her." He added the suggestion that Clara should become a schoolteacher.

Mrs. Barton was startled at the idea of her timid Clara being a teacher, but she was impressed by

Mr. Fowler's advice—and so was Clara. The family accepted the idea gratefully and without argument. Clara seems to have accepted it with only one thought:

"If I am going to be a teacher, I will be a good one."

With this in mind, she continued school for another year, and then applied for a certificate to teach in a little one-room school across town. It was very near where her married sister, Sally, was living.

A certificate to teach in those days did not mean going to a teachers college, or any college. It meant an examination before a clergyman, a lawyer and a justice of the peace.

For once, Clara was not afraid, but she made every effort to appear older and taller than she was. She did her hair high on her head, lengthened her skirts, hoped she looked more than seventeen, and presented herself demurely on The Day.

She passed the examination with a rating of excellent, and found herself with nothing to do until the beginning of the spring school term. There was plenty of time to worry herself into a panic about facing a class, and she would most certainly have made herself ill with fright if David hadn't chosen that time to get married.

He was marrying a Maine girl and the wedding would, of course, be in her home. Clara went to Maine with David, had the time of her life, and was distracted from her fears for a while anyway.

They returned the moment she was back in Oxford, but there was not much time left for her to work herself up again. She worked desperately preparing a little opening speech to be delivered to her class, which was rapidly assuming in her mind the quality of a many-headed monster.

She moved to Sally's, where she was to live. The day came.

If ever anyone could be described as "scared

green," it was Miss Clara H. Barton, aged seven-
teen-and-a-half, when she arrived in the school-
yard.

It was empty.

Her hand shook as she opened the schoolhouse
door, and she paused, literally paralyzed, on the
threshold.

Forty pairs of eyes were staring at her, un-
blinking, in a dead silence. She stared back,
numb with fright.

There were boys and girls of all ages and sizes,
including four big boys almost as old as Clara.
She had heard of these four. They were strong,
they were tough, they were mean. They had
locked the previous teacher out of the schoolhouse and had taken possession of it themselves.
Their eyes, fixed on Clara's face, were hard and
challenging.

Somehow she made her way to the teacher's
desk. Her carefully prepared speech vanished
from her mind as if it had never been. Luckily,

Clara had heard about the four mean boys in her class

there was a Bible on the desk. She picked it up,
and it fell open at the fifth chapter of Matthew.
She heard with astonishment her own voice reading the immortal and familiar beatitudes and her
courage came back with a rush.

When she reached the seventh, "Blessed are
the merciful for they shall obtain mercy," she

glanced involuntarily at the four boys. They looked away.

Clara breathed again, and her voice was suddenly strong and clear. She read to the end. Then, confidently, she began her classes. The four boys did nothing to disturb the peace.

During the noon lunch hour Clara went out on the playground. There was a ball game in progress. Clara, blessing David for having taught her to pitch a fast ball, joined in the game. The four boys grinned joyfully at one another, but within ten minutes their grins had vanished.

The new teacher could pitch a ball much better than they could, and she could run like a deer. They tried other games, and found that Clara was stronger than they were. If the big boys won in anything, it was because Clara let them—and they knew it. The challenge in their eyes was gone, and in its place were respect and admiration.

Before the first week was over, the four had taken to hanging around after school with offers

to help. They ran errands. They cleaned black-
boards. They swept. They brought in wood for
the stove. They carried her books home for her.

Rumors of this model behavior began to spread
through the village, and Clara found herself with
a reputation for discipline.

She was indignant.

"There has been no discipline!" she protested.
"I haven't disciplined anybody!"

Seventy long years afterward one of those boys
said that he could still remember the white flash
of Clara's teeth when she smiled.

Clara says simply, "They were faithful to me in
school and faithful later to their country, for their
blood crimsoned some of the hardest battlefields.
I have never seen finer boys."

5

Woman's Place

Clara's self-confidence and her success as a teacher grew. Her reputation as a disciplinarian continued. She was often "borrowed" for part of a term to take over some nearby school in which the teacher had been having trouble. Clara never had any trouble with her youngsters and could not understand why anyone else did. She was convinced that the trouble was mostly imaginary.

Meanwhile, Stephen and David bought a factory. When Clara discovered that the "mill children" were getting no education, she started a school for them and taught in it for a number of years, living at home.

Her agonizing shyness, which came and went all her life, almost disappeared during this period. She was busy, happy and popular. She enjoyed herself thoroughly with young people her own age.

Clara was not considered a pretty girl according to the standards of that day. She had beautiful, dark, glossy hair, fine brown eyes, a straight, strong nose, and a wide, sensitive mouth. Today she would be considered a handsome woman. Even then she was obviously attractive, for during the ten years in which she was teaching in and around Oxford a number of young men tried earnestly to persuade her to marry them.

One of these, having been refused, rushed madly

off to California, determined to make a fortune in the gold rush and dazzle Clara into marrying him.

He actually did make a fortune, and returned in triumph to Clara.

Unfortunately for him, Clara was not in the least dazzled. She was deeply touched, but she still said, "No." Desperate, and in spite of Clara's flat refusal to permit such a thing, he deposited ten thousand dollars to her account in the bank. She wouldn't touch it. He wouldn't have it back. So it remained there, comfortably accumulating interest, a very decided tribute to Clara's charm.

Charm is difficult to explain because there are so many different kinds. A friend who once crossed the Atlantic on the same boat with Clara has tried to describe the effect which Clara had on most people.

"Miss Barton had extraordinary magnetism. It was her eyes, I think. She had the warmest, most sympathetic, understanding eyes I've ever en-

countered in my whole life. When she looked at
you, she seemed to know exactly what you were
thinking and how you felt. She was very witty
and she liked to laugh—but it wasn't that; it was
the way she made you feel. It was wonderful! I
remember that she nearly always wore red, a lovely
deep, soft red, and it seems to me that she had
dark brown hair. I *know* it wasn't white, though
she must have been in her seventies at the time. I
suppose she was tiny, but you didn't think much
about her appearance or her size, or what age she
might be—they didn't matter. She looked at you
with those eyes and smiled—and you were sunk."

Clara's eyes could sink people in quite a different way. Those who were selfish, dishonest,
and spiteful didn't like Clara, or her clear eyes
which, however kind, saw too much. For such
people Clara had no charm whatever. In later years
she made enemies, only a few at first, then in increasing numbers as she became famous.

In 1850, when she was twenty-nine years old,

she began to think that she would be a better teacher if she knew more. She decided to go to college and take a year of special courses. She chose the Liberal Institute, which was a part of Hamilton College in Clinton, New York.

This was a long way from home in days when travel was slow. It was almost three days' journey from Oxford, and this suited Clara's plan. She did not propose to be called back home every time some teacher imagined herself in difficulties.

The family was startled and distressed, particularly her brothers. They leaned heavily on Clara's good business judgment and common sense, but as they approved of her purpose in going they had to give in as gracefully as possible.

Stephen and David drove her to the station and waved until the train was out of sight. This time they felt that Clara was really going out into the world. How far she was going her brothers could not have dreamed.

The year in college gave Clara what she wanted,

educationally, and brought her a new lifelong friend in Mary Norton, another student, from Bordentown, New Jersey. It was a friendship which was to have an unexpected effect on Bordentown.

That year also brought her a severe shock, for her mother died suddenly. Clara could not get home in time for the funeral, and the family urged her to remain where she was.

Clara was stunned with grief. It was her first encounter with death. She was unable to imagine home, or the world, without her mother, but she was not her mother's daughter for nothing. Mrs. Barton would have said, "Go on with your work." Clara went on with it as best she could, comforted by Mary Norton's kindness and sympathy.

There were other problems as well. Two young men who were teaching at the college fell in love with her. What she was to do with them she didn't know. One she nearly married and her friendship with him continued for some years, but in the end she refused him as she had refused all the others.

It is not, of course, an unbearable hardship for any girl to have two very nice boys in love with her at the same time. But Clara was neither vain nor silly, and she didn't like hurting anyone. Besides, she didn't really want to get married, so she was more distressed than gratified by the situation.

When her course was finished, she went home, to find everything sadly changed. Her mother was gone. The house was closed. Her father was living with Stephen and his family. There was nothing to keep Clara there now, so after a brief stay she went to visit Mary Norton in Bordentown.

She went to spend a few weeks and stayed for ten years—teaching in the Bordentown schools. Here she started the first public school in the state of New Jersey.

This came about in a particularly Clara-Barton manner.

As she went for her customary walks around the town, she noticed that there were many more children out of school than in. She made inquiries and learned that these were children whose parents could not afford the price of admission to the local private schools.

There were no other schools. Although the state had splendid public school laws, none of them had ever been enforced. Boys of all ages were idling on the street corners or hanging around the saloons. Clara lost no time in getting acquainted with as many as possible—an easy matter, for she liked and understood boys.

It was not long before they were talking to her freely of their problems, their hopes, and their bitterness because they could not get an education.

"Lady, there's no school for kids like us," they told her. "We'd be thankful to go if there was one."

When Clara had heard this a dozen times in one afternoon, she blew up. She went straight to Mr. Suydam, chairman of the school committee, and announced that she wished to open a public school for these boys and their sisters. She would teach in it herself.

Mr. Suydam was startled, sympathetic and upset. He assured her that it was a splendid idea, but impossible. The boys were juvenile delinquents, he said. A woman could do nothing with them. They wouldn't go to school if they had a chance. Anyway, their parents wouldn't send them to a "pauper school." The boys came from bad homes and the respectable people of the town would be shocked at the idea of a *woman* having anything to do with such people or their children. Her reputation would be ruined. And who would pay her salary? She had better give up the whole thing at once—forget about it.

Clara listened and said nothing. She merely looked at him. Mr. Suydam wiped his forehead. There was silence. At last Clara said:

"Thank you, Mr. Suydam. Shall I speak?"

He laughed in spite of himself. "Certainly, Miss Barton."

She took the objections one by one. She had been, she explained, a public schoolteacher for years in Massachusetts. She was accustomed to dealing with all kinds of children. She knew boys. She knew *these* boys and was not in the least afraid of them. As for her reputation, she thought it was good enough to stand a little criticism, though she didn't want, or intend, to stir up local prejudice. All she wanted was to open a school where these outcast children could go and be taught. And she didn't want a salary. She would be glad to teach these children for nothing.

Mr. Suydam was unable to find an answer to any of this and was silent. Clara continued.

The school, she stated positively, must have the backing of the law and the school board *as officers of the law*. The board must produce a building, furnish it, and give the townspeople due notice of what was going on. The school, in fact, *must exist by their order* and a town school could not be considered a pauper school.

"You can leave the work and the results to me," she said. "I'm not looking for anything for my-self. I only want to use the force of a good and established state law against ignorance and prej-udice."

Perhaps the public education of children wouldn't work, she concluded, but at least the people had a right to find out by seeing it tried. *And* there was already a building—an old schoolhouse long since closed. It could be re-paired and reopened.

Clara had overlooked nothing, missed no point.

Mr. Suydam looked at her with profound re-spect. Then he said abruptly, "I will lay the mat-ter before the school board at once."

Clara got her school.

It opened with six pupils. At the end of a year there were six hundred, and a large new school had been built for them. The town was bursting with pride—a pride that was the beginning of trou-ble for Clara.

6

Injustice

Clara had started the school, had developed it, had run it expertly. When the new building was ready, her thrilled pupils assumed that Clara would be principal.

It is doubtful if Clara had given the matter any great amount of thought. She was not looking for honors; she never did. But the school, after all, was her own in a very special way, and she loved it. She must have expected to be named principal.

At this point the prejudice of which Mr. Suydam had warned her began to make itself felt. There were many people, as he had said, who still clung to the idea that a woman is incapable of holding a responsible position. They were sincerely grateful to Clara, but they did not want her to be principal of such a big, such a very *important* new school. They insisted that it was now too large for a woman to handle.

Clara had made it large, and she had been handling it with the utmost efficiency. Prejudice, however, pays no attention to facts. A few narrow-minded old fogies started the uproar.

People of the same opinion, who had been too timid to express it before, now spoke up loudly. Others joined the chorus because it seemed to be the thing to do, and they didn't want to be on the wrong side.

Clara, who would fight for someone else until

she dropped, made no effort to fight for herself. The opposition won, and a man was hired as principal. Clara accepted him with quiet courtesy, though she had been deeply hurt.

If the new principal had been a person with any strength of mind, generosity, or fairness, everything would have been all right. Unfortunately he was weak and vain.

It didn't take him long to discover that, however unjust the townspeople had been to Clara, they liked, admired and respected her. To make matters worse, he found that Clara was far more capable than he was, and he determined to get rid of her by any means.

At first he was cautious, confining himself to being disagreeable and sneering in his manner with Clara. Then, as she did nothing about it, he took courage and began to find fault with her work. Nothing she did suited him. If she had to be severe with a pupil, he sided with the pupil. He began to criticize her methods, first to the other teachers and then publicly around the town. He tried his best to throw discredit on Clara, and he must have found it difficult, if not almost impossible. But he did manage to make the sensitive Clara's life miserable.

She could have resigned, of course, but she had no wish to be run out of her school in such a way. He had no power to fire her. The situation grew steadily worse, and the strain wore Clara to the point of exhaustion. She grew thin and pale and wrote Stephen that she had been half sick all winter.

In her run-down condition it is not surprising that she lost her voice. The surprising thing is that it did not come back. One cannot teach without a voice. Clara resigned thankfully and, in a state of nervous collapse, went home. Her voice did not return, and she went to Washington, D.C., hoping that the warmer climate would help her throat.

The school in which she first taught in Bordentown is now a memorial to her.

The weak principal was determined to get rid of Clara

7

Washington in 1854

Clara Barton was thirty-two years old when she went to Washington, and she had not the faintest idea of giving up her career as a teacher. She merely felt that she needed a rest, a milder climate for her throat, and a chance to learn, first-hand, a little about the nation's politics.

It is difficult, now, to imagine Washington as

it was when Clara arrived in 1854. Then it was
an untidy city of slightly more than 50,000 people.
The city had been beautifully planned and laid
out, but the building of it had barely begun.
Streets and sidewalks were unpaved, swirling dust
in summer and spattering mud in winter. There
were few street lights, and the water system was
largely imaginary. Drinking water still came from
wells and springs. The parks and squares had already been laid out according to the plan, but no
one took care of them and they were overrun
with weeds and tall grass.

Still, it was the nation's capital, and Clara was
fascinated. After New Jersey and Massachusetts
it seemed very warm, and she was sure her throat
would improve. She rented a room and settled
down, spending as much time as she could in the
Senate and House, listening to Congressional debates.

This occupied her very nicely until her voice
began to improve and her energy returned. Then

The resentful men made remarks as Clara Barton passed

she grew restless, and as she was not yet ready to plunge back into teaching she decided to look around for some kind of work, full or part time.

This took her to Colonel Alexander De Witt, an old friend of her father's and Congressman from her home district. She had known him since she was a child. Now she asked him to suggest something for her to do—something which would not require much use of her voice.

He introduced her to the man who was then head of the Patent Office, Judge Charles Mason. Judge Mason liked Clara and offered her a job as clerk in his department.

She was one of the first women employed in a government department to do a man's work at a man's pay, and most of the men were furiously resentful. They took it out in being as unpleasant as possible, lining up in the corridor to stare and grin and make remarks as she passed. They blew smoke in her face and spat tobacco juice as close to her as they dared. One even started a slanderous story about her and took it to Judge Mason, whose only reply was:

"Prove what you are saying. If you are right, she goes. If wrong, you go." It was the man who lost his job.

Clara steadily ignored all of this, and in time the

men grew tired of the game and let her alone.

During that first year in Washington, her brother Stephen bought two thousand acres of land in North Carolina and moved there to set up a lumber mill. He left Clara feeling very bleak. Stephen had been her champion since she was born. Much as she loved David, it was to Stephen that she took all her problems. North Carolina seemed very far away.

She missed him even more at the beginning of her second year in Washington, for she was having trouble with the Secretary of the Interior, Robert McClelland. This was in no way Clara's fault, but was due to the fact that she had been given her job by Judge Mason. Mr. McClelland did not like Judge Mason and had been interfering with him at every turn. When the Secretary suddenly decided that it was most improper for women to work in a public office with men, Clara nearly lost her job. Colonel De Witt interceded for her and she didn't lose it.

She stayed on grimly, and the matter was finally dropped.

Ultimately Judge Mason resigned. Then James Buchanan was elected President of the United States, and Mr. McClelland was replaced. Clara worked on, undisturbed, for another year. Then the government decided to cut expenses, and a great many people found themselves out of jobs, including Clara.

She went home without regret.

Nevertheless, the years in Washington had done much for her in ways which would be invaluable to her later.

She made a great many friends among the Congressmen and their wives, and they were impressed by her level-headedness and capability. The hours spent in listening to Congressional debates were not wasted, either, for by the time Clara went home she was one of the best informed women in the country, politically. In addition, and quite unknown to herself, Clara's quick, observant mind had missed no trick of oratory, no skillful method of presenting an argument or making a speech.

Now she was glad to find herself at home once more. For three years she remained there, happy to be with her father, who was now eighty-three and not very well. Also, it was her first long rest— and her last for years to come.

She kept in touch with national affairs while she was at home, and she worried about the growing quarrels between the Northern and Southern states. The country was slowly but surely drifting toward a war between the states, a civil war. Clara could not believe that the North and the South would really fight each other or that, if they did, it would amount to anything. But it was impossible not to be alarmed by the situation.

Meanwhile her excellent work at the Patent Office, combined with her already well-known ability, was being missed in Washington. Suddenly

she was called back to the Patent Office just before Abraham Lincoln became President of the
United States.

Clara was pleased, of course, that her good work
in the Patent Office had been recognized, but still
she hesitated. She had seriously considered becoming a teacher again and was not at all sure that
she wanted to go back to Washington, with all
its turmoil.

Her father urged her to go, and Clara had always trusted her father's judgment.

The autumn of 1860 found her back at her
desk in the Patent Office with scarcely a breath
to spare before civil war burst upon the horrified
nation.

8

War Begins

The deep-down, real beginning of the trouble between the Northern and Southern states came from the fact that over a period of many years they had developed such different ways of life. They lived differently, thought differently, and no longer understood each other's ways.

The North had developed rapidly and with

great energy. It had factories, railroads, steamship lines, all kinds of industries. Also it had almost twice the population of the South.

The South was farming country. It had only about one-fifth of the nation's factories, few railroads, and its population had scarcely increased at all. The two crops upon which the South depended were cotton and tobacco, and the South was a network of great plantations, with slaves to do the work. The rich plantation owners lived a peaceful, charming life, very different from the bustle and hurry of the North.

During the ten years before the Civil War, over two million persons had come to the United States from Europe. They had little or no money and needed work to live. There was no work for them in the South, where everything was done by slave labor, so they settled in the North and East. Then, as the West opened up, with its promise of free land, they moved west where new states were being created, one by one.

People in these new states did not want slaves who would take the work away from them. They wanted a guarantee that all would be free. Their states were known as "Free States." Southerners feared that there would be more Free States than "Slave States." This might put the North in the position of being able to tell the South what it could or could not do in any matter which came to a vote in Congress.

The South, naturally, didn't like this. Furthermore, it wanted more land to extend its plantations and its slave system. There was no more land except in the new states and in the Utah and New Mexico Territories where the climate was unsuitable.

The South began to think about separating from the Union and having its own government, so that it would be independent of the North, where the great majority of the people opposed the idea. America was still a young country and not very strong as yet. To separate the states, making two nations, would weaken both, and if any powerful foreign country wished to attack either—both might be lost. The states, united, were better off than divided.

The South didn't think so. It felt, and said, that each state had a right to do as it pleased—go or stay.

More and more quarrels arose about states' rights and about slavery. Some leaders in the North had been shouting that nobody should have slaves. Others believed that slavery should be limited to states where it already existed. Many in the South wanted to remain in the Union but thought that each state should have the right to make its own decisions.

When Lincoln was elected President in 1860, South Carolina withdrew from the Union. A month later Georgia, Alabama, Florida, Louisiana and Mississippi seceded, followed shortly by Texas. In February, 1861, representatives of the seceding states met in Montgomery, Alabama, and set up a new nation, the Confederated States of America. They elected their own President and Congress. As these states withdrew from the Union, some of them seized the Union shipyards, forts, arsenals, or other public property within their borders.

The North and the South were now so furious with each other that everyone knew war was inevitable.

It came all too soon. Union soldiers were stationed in Fort Sumter, at Charleston, South Carolina—one of the new Confederate states. South Carolina demanded the fort. President Lincoln said, "No!" Confederate soldiers attacked the fort and captured it. Then the border states of North Carolina, Virginia, Arkansas and Tennessee joined the Confederacy. And the War Between the States, the Civil War, had begun.

It was a tragic and dreadful thing. It lasted four years, a million young men were killed or wounded, and the South was in ruins.

There were Southern sympathizers in the North

and Northern sympathizers in the South. Brother turned against brother, sons against their fathers.

Clara Barton was still in Bordentown, New Jersey, when the early rumblings and quarrels began. Like many people, she did not pay much attention at first. When she went to Washington, however, she began to realize that the trouble was serious.

The trouble grew worse every month during the time she was at home. Even before she returned to Washington, she was begging Stephen to leave North Carolina.

Stephen was in his fifties then, and he had spent his entire fortune on his property and industries in North Carolina. If he left, it would be seized. Besides, he was too old for service in the Union Army and he did not believe the war would last long anyway. He would stay where he was and protect his property, and the family was not to worry.

Clara, too, thought that the war would not last

long, but after the fall of Fort Sumter she was caught up in the rising tide of excitement. Her childhood longing to be a soldier came back to her. Everywhere young men were rushing into uniform. Bands were playing. Flags were flying.

"Well," Clara thought, "since I can't very well be a soldier, I can at least go to the front and nurse the wounded."

How she was to get to the front she didn't know, for at that time there was *not one trained nurse in the whole United States*, nor was there even the beginning of a nursing school anywhere.

Women with a gift for nursing got experience in the same way that Clara had—by nursing relatives, friends or neighbors, and by learning all they could from the family doctor.

Throughout the Civil War, women from both North and South worked tirelessly and heroically in the base hospitals, but few ever saw the front unless the front came to them. A battlefield was not considered a suitable place for women.

Clara regarded it as highly suitable. She was accustomed to being told that almost anything she was doing or wished to do was not proper for a woman. But so far, no one had been able to keep her from doing it. Clara Barton never did any important thing hastily. Now she waited, planning, considering, making inquiries. Her first service to her country in war had nothing to do with nursing.

The newly created Confederate Army was streaming north through Virginia and Maryland, hoping to capture Washington. The Union Army was streaming south to block them, and hoping to capture Richmond, the Confederate capital.

The Sixth Massachusetts Regiment, recruited from Worcester and the villages around it—including Oxford—was the first to reach Washington. They had been attacked by Southern sympathizers in Baltimore and reached Washington battered, hungry, and with all baggage lost. There were no tents for them so they were quartered in the Cap-

itol itself, sleeping in rows on the floor of the
Senate Chamber.

Clara knew that there would be friends, and
probably ex-pupils, among them. She went to find
out what she could do for them. The only com-
plaint of the soldiers was that they were all roast-
ing in long woolen underwear. Clara vanished and
did not return until the following morning. Then
she brought with her five Negro porters staggering under boxes of cotton underwear and food.

"Can I do anything else for you?" she asked.

A quick-eyed young soldier pointed to the
Worcester newspaper under Clara's arm. It was
his hometown paper.

"Would you mind reading us that?"

She laughed. "That's what I brought it for," she
said and mounted the steps to the Vice-President's
desk. Standing there, she read the paper aloud to
them. The once shy and timid Clara Barton faced
hundreds of eyes without a quiver, her voice

ringing out strong and clear across the vast Senate Chamber.

The men cheered her wildly when she had finished.

Clara went home and notified the Worcester papers that she would receive stores, supplies, and money for the wounded of the Sixth Massachusetts Regiment. She agreed to give them out herself, wherever the regiment might be.

In that one stroke she had arranged to get herself to the front, she thought.

9

Where There's a Will

But getting to the front was not to be as easy as
Clara expected. She had to have permission and
passes from the War Department in order to go
to the front, and this involved a great many officials. Some were willing, but more were not. If
there had been a series of terrible battles immediately after the declaration of war, Clara would

undoubtedly have received permission to go. But in spite of the suddenness with which the war started, it was slow in working up to heavy, sustained fighting.

Jefferson Davis, President of the Confederate States, counted on the support of France and England to help him. Because he believed that the war would soon be over, he did not force any battles.

The North was not prepared for war. Its army was tiny and poorly equipped. Men had to be recruited in hundreds of thousands, then equipped, then trained. Many of its best officers were Southerners who resigned their commissions to join the Confederate Army. President Abraham Lincoln still hoped for a peaceful settlement.

In addition to all this, neither army knew exactly where the other was. It must be remembered that there were no planes, no radios, no telephones, no automobiles. The telegraph had been invented, but it wasn't always handy and didn't always work.

Information about troop movements was carried
to headquarters and to Washington on foot or on
horseback. The armies were like two blind bears
fumbling for each other.

It is not surprising, therefore, that during the
next twelve months there was only one battle of
any size, the First Battle of Bull Run, sometimes
called the First Battle of Manassas. It ended in
defeat for the Union forces.

Clara did not know the extent of the battle until it was over, but she helped nurse the wounded
who were brought back to Washington hospitals.
The soldiers' stories made her realize more than
ever that nurses were needed on the battlefield itself.

Army supplies followed the marching troops
in slow lumbering wagons. The supply train was
miles, and often *days*, behind. There were surgeons to operate on the worst of the wounded—
provided the medical supplies arrived in time. The
wounded were carted away in the same kind of

slow wagons, to the nearest railway or boat landing or town, usually without food, water or medical care. Their suffering was appalling.

Many who could have been saved bled to death in the jolting wagons because their wounds had not been dressed. Many others died on the battlefield, not of their wounds alone, but of thirst and exposure.

Clara Barton was determined to get permission to go to the front as a nurse. She bombarded the War Department with her demands. She fought prejudice, unreasoning obstinacy and plain stupidity. The War Department insisted that the army was well supplied with everything, and that it did not need nurses, male or female.

Meanwhile, small clashes and skirmishes took place and the soldiers continued to die of sickness, wounds or hunger. For lack of blankets in that "well-supplied" army, the wounded froze to the ground in winter.

Clara fought on. She went to the governor of

Massachusetts, who was solidly on her side. She wrote to the head chaplain of the army. She made a friend of the Assistant Quartermaster-General, Colonel Rucker, who was in command of supplies and in a position to give her transportation. She continued to collect supplies until she had to rent a warehouse to hold them, and she carried them to any troops she could reach. She was becoming very well-known, and the soldiers adored her.

Exactly what finally turned the tide in her favor is not known, but something or somebody did. Unknown to Clara, who had been called home to her dying father, the various passes were signed.

Captain Barton died in March, 1862, with David, Clara, and Sally at his bedside. There was no word of Stephen. No one knew what was happening to him. Captain Barton was a very old man, and Clara had been prepared for his death. She could not wish him to live any longer.

On the day of the funeral the army passes came, with permission from the Surgeon General of the

Union Army to go to the front with the Army of the Potomac. Clara Barton was to be given whatever she needed in the way of transportation or other assistance in caring for the wounded. She could go to any part of the front so long as it was with the Army of the Potomac. She could take with her anyone she could get to help her.

Such an extraordinary pass would be impossible today. It left Clara a completely free agent to go and come as she pleased, and under nobody's orders but her own.

It seemed too good to be true.

The combination of her father's funeral and the arrival of this glorious overall permission from the Surgeon General was too much. Clara, who rarely cried, burst into tears.

10

Second Battle of Bull Run

Clara's first year of active service in the army was important not only in what she did but also in what she learned. Both North and South now realized that the war would not be over soon, that no foreign country would help either side, and that the only way to end the war was to fight it to a finish. The Confederates still wanted Washington;

the Union still wanted Richmond. That second year of the war was one of hard battles in Virginia and Maryland.

Clara was present at nearly every one and from each she learned something more, until her work became skillful and well organized.

Her first really tough lesson came at the Second Battle of Bull Run, in September of 1862, near Fairfax, Virginia. There three thousand wounded and ravenous men lay crowded on a slope close to the Fairfax railroad station. The battle itself was going on about two miles away, near a small stream named Bull Run. Clara found that bales of hay had been broken open and the hay spread over the ground. The wounded were lying on this.

Clara had brought another woman with her, a Mrs. Fales. Without wasting a moment, they gathered up all that they had in the way of kitchen equipment. When it was assembled, they stared at each other, horrified.

They had two water buckets, five tin cups, one camp kettle, one stewpan, two lanterns, four bread knives, three plates, and a two-quart tin dish. And there were three thousand men to feed!

In writing of this later, to a friend, Clara said:

"I had not yet learned to equip myself, but grew into my work by hard thinking and sad experience. . . . I assure you that I was never so caught again."

She continued, "You have read of adverse winds. To realize this in its fullest sense you have only to build a campfire and attempt to cook something on it. There is not a soldier but will sustain me in the assertion that, go whichsoever side of it you will, wind will blow smoke in your face. Notwithstanding these difficulties, within fifteen minutes from the time of our arrival we were preparing food and dressing wounds. You wonder what, and how prepared, and how administered without dishes."

One might well wonder. Clara's practical mind

and quick common sense solved the problem. Beside the railroad tracks were the tons of preserves and fruit sent to Clara by wives and mothers.

"Huge boxes of these stood waiting. Every can, jar, bucket, bowl, cup or tumbler, when emptied, became a vehicle of mercy to carry mingled bread and wine, soup, or coffee to some helpless sufferer. . . . I never realized until that day how little a human being could be grateful for."

By this time she also realized the foolishness of taking anything to the front which could not be used to good purpose once it got there, though only experience would teach her all that would be needed.

They toiled all day in the hot sun, but worse was coming with the night. Clara describes it.

"I have said that the ground was littered with dry hay, and that we had only two lanterns, but there were plenty of candles. The wounded were laid so close that it was impossible to move about in the dark. The slightest misstep brought a torrent of groans from some poor mangled soldier.

"Consequently, here were seen persons of all grades, from the careful man of God who walked with a prayer upon his lips to the careless teamster hunting for his lost whip—each wandering about among this hay with an open, flaming candle in his hand.

"The slightest accident, the mere dropping of a light could have enveloped in flames this whole mass of helpless men. We watched and pleaded and cautioned as we worked that night. . . . We put socks and slippers on cold damp feet, wrapped your quilts and blankets around them and when we no longer had these to give we covered them with hay.

"On Monday the enemy cavalry appeared in the wood opposite and a raid was hourly expected. In the afternoon all the wounded men were sent off and the danger became so imminent that Mrs. Fales thought best to leave, though she only went for stores. I begged to be excused from accompanying her, as the wagons were up to the fields for more, and I knew that I should never leave a wounded man there, if I were taken prisoner forty times.

"At six o'clock it commenced to thunder and lighten, and all at once the artillery began to play, joined by the distant musketry. We sat down in our tent and waited to see them break through but the old 21st Massachusetts lay between us and the enemy and they could not pass. . . . Next day all fell back. We put the thousand wounded men we then had into the train and steamed off."

The day they "steamed off" was Tuesday. Clara had had one and a half hours' sleep since Saturday, but at the end of her letter she says firmly that she is well and strong and ready to go again.

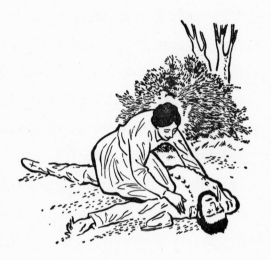

11

Chantilly

Nurses at the front today wear coveralls and are not hampered by skirts but in Clara's time a woman in any kind of trousers was the object of ridicule. Those were the days of hoop skirts and ruffles. Even a woman working in her own kitchen wore a skirt lined with stiff crinoline to make it stand out. All skirts touched the ground. It was considered immodest for a woman to show her ankles.

Clara's battle dress was a plain black jacket and a skirt with no stiffening in it. It hung straight down her slim figure, and it did not quite touch the ground. This was all she could manage in the way of sensible clothes. The only personal articles she took with her were such as could be wrapped up in a single handkerchief.

The Battle of Chantilly was another defeat for the Union Army, and took place very near Bull Run. In fact, Clara found herself right back again at Fairfax Station, this time with two other women whose names she doesn't mention, and ample equipment in the way of camp kettles, pails and boxes of lanterns.

The battle had already begun when Clara arrived. She was two miles distant from the actual fighting, and she felt again that she could save more lives if she were nearer. However, there was no way to get there, and the wounded were already being brought in.

The three women had begun work when Clara noticed a soldier with a mangled right arm lying on the ground near by. His shirt was half off, and he was shivering. Clara went over to him and bent to pull his shirt across his bare chest when he startled her by flinging his good arm around her neck and bursting into tears. Clara took his head in her hands and held it until he was quiet.

"Don't you know me?" he asked. "I used to carry your books home from school."

He was one of the four "bad" boys from her very first school, and Clara remarked sadly that that arm would never carry any more books.

They worked all night, as usual. About three o'clock in the morning a surgeon with a candle in his hand appeared in search of Clara.

"Lady," he said, "will you come with me? Up on the hill is a poor distressed lad, mortally wounded. His cries for his sister have touched all our hearts, and none of us can relieve him."

Clara followed him at once, toiling up the hillside to where a flickering of candles clustered in a group. She could already hear the cries of the delirious man. "Mary! Mary! Sister, come! Don't let me die here alone." He did not seem aware of the men around him.

Clara found him stretched out on the ground in the candlelight, his bloody hands clasped against his chest, his eyes turning piteously from side to side. Clara motioned the men away until she could kneel beside him in the darkness, hoping he would believe her to be his sister. Then she took his hands and kissed him gently on the forehead.

He cried out joyfully. "Mary! I knew you'd come! I knew it! I'm not afraid to die now. Bless you, Mary!"

Clara gave him a stimulant, wrapped him in a blanket, and sitting down on the ground lifted his head and shoulders into her lap, where she put her warm arms around him. He fell asleep at once. Clara sat there for three hours, while the warmth came slowly back into the boy's cold body.

It was dawn when he woke, no longer delirious, but puzzled. He looked up at Clara. "I—I know now she couldn't get here," he said slowly. "Who —is it?"

"Just a woman who came to help you," she told him, and called to the surgeon.

When the young soldier was safely on the train, Clara went back to work.

In a letter to a friend she says, "Although three hours of my time had been devoted to one sufferer among thousands, you must not think that the work stopped or that my assistants had been equally inefficient. They doubled their efforts in making up for my deficiencies."

They worked all day while wagons by the hundred brought in the wounded. Most of the men were already weak from hunger and loss of blood, yet it would be another twenty-four hours before they would be in a hospital or would get any nourishment. If they were taken from the wagons and put on the ground among the men already cared for, they would surely be overlooked.

Clara went to the officers on the grounds with a suggestion to which they agreed at once. Orders were sent out that all wagons were to stop at a given point and not move on until their wounded had been seen and fed.

So all that day Clara climbed from the ground to the wheel to the brake of each wagon, as it stopped. She fed every wounded man until he was satisfied and then dressed his wounds. How many lives she saved by this intelligent idea will never be known.

Late in the afternoon when there was a lull, Clara and her assistants gathered around a box to snatch a little food themselves, for they had eaten nothing since the day before. At this moment artillery fire, the Confederate cavalry, a thunderstorm, and another long wagon train of wounded appeared all at once.

It is hardly necessary to say that the three women did not finish their meal.

The Union cavalry was able to hold back the Confederates for a time, at least, and the women worked on in torrents of rain and a deafening uproar. The lightning flashed and so did the artillery. Presently Clara's assistants gave out. One climbed aboard the waiting train. The other crawled into Clara's tent and went to sleep. Clara worked on alone in the downpour until the last trainload of wounded had pulled out of the station. The guns were suddenly quiet.

Clara's tent was pitched in a little hollow on the hillside. She moved stiffly toward it, sliding and falling in the pitch darkness, pushed aside the tent flap and stepped in—to a "well-established" brook which was flowing briskly across the floor. Her remaining assistant was asleep on top of the only box in the tent.

There was no spot where Clara could lie down and sleep except in the brook, and in the brook she slept.

She says that at first she tried to keep her head

propped up somehow, so that the water wouldn't flow into her ears, but after a time she abandoned the effort, and let it flow. She slept for two hours, woke greatly "rested and strengthened," wrung the water out of her hair and clothes, and went out.

Another wagon train of wounded was rumbling toward her. The rain had stopped and the guns were still silent, but she was told that the Confederate cavalry was on the prowl close by.

Clara put her exhausted assistant on the train to look after the wounded there, and went back to work alone, expecting capture at any minute. As she moved slowly forward among the wounded, she went farther and farther from the station until it grew tiny in the distance.

Toward dawn a Union cavalry officer galloped up.

"Miss Barton, can you ride?"

"Yes, sir."

Clara galloped off to catch the departing wagon train

"But you have no lady's saddle. Could you ride mine?"

"Yes, sir, or without it," said the woman who had ridden wild colts bareback over her father's acres.

The officer was relieved. "Then you can risk

another hour of work," he said, and, promising to come back, galloped away.

Clara worked at top speed, determined to get every wounded man on the train. The last one had just been removed to safety when the officer came back at frantic speed. As he flung himself from his horse, Clara saw the Confederate cavalry pouring down the hillside toward her.

"Try for the train," the officer urged. "It's going right out. If you can't make it, you'll have to take a chance on escaping across country."

Clara made it in two minutes flat.

12

Flank Movement

After the Battle of Chantilly, Clara had a scant week's rest in Washington before she heard that a battle was to take place at Harpers Ferry, eighty miles away, in West Virginia. She knew that the information might be wrong, but it was all she had. She left at once with her mule team of supplies, jolting and jouncing over the rough roads all day, and camping where night found her. There were no women with her—only the four men whom Colonel Rucker had sent her as guard and escort.

Her information was wrong. There was no battle at Harpers Ferry, but a small one had already taken place farther on. Along the way Clara met the walking wounded and stragglers from the battle. Some wore uniforms of the Union blue, others of Confederate gray. They were exhausted and hungry and Clara fed them all alike as she passed, renewing her supplies at every village.

Next morning, however, she overtook a Union wagon train. It was ten miles long, and carried ammunition, food, clothing, and medical supplies. From its size Clara knew that it was surely going to some impending battle. Very well, she would go with it. She followed it all day in a smother of heat and dust, unable to pass it on the narrow road. When it pulled over for the night, Clara stopped, too, and made camp.

Long after everyone was asleep, Clara was still awake in her wagon, staring up at the stars and listening to the night sounds. They were peaceful sounds: the whisper of leaves, the jingle of a chain, the snap of a spark, and the thin far-off barking of a dog. A wisp of campfire smoke came to her on the night wind.

She lay tense in the starlight, praying for a Union victory. So far there had been only defeats. And what could she do, so far back—ten miles back of everything when she should be far ahead?

She thought of her father, that wise old soldier who could surely have told her what to do. Suddenly she remembered the war games of her childhood, played on the living-room rug at home. She saw again the grains of yellow corn, two lines facing each other. She saw her father's hands, moving his pieces around one end of hers.

She sat up.

"Flank movement!" she said aloud, and scrambled out of the wagon smiling, to wake her men.

"We're going on," she told them.

They were stupefied with sleep, but if she could take it, they could. They stumbled out of their blankets and harnessed the protesting mules while Clara made coffee.

All the remainder of that night their wagon lumbered and jingled past the sleeping wagon train. At daybreak they passed the foremost wagon, and the road was clear. All day the hot September sun blistered them, but at dusk she reached the Army of the Potomac, eighty thousand men along Antietam Creek. Clara's campfire made one more among the thousands.

"Now," she told herself, "I shall follow the cannon."

13

Antietam

Antietam was the first great Union victory and one of the worst battles of the war. Along an eight-mile front 124,000 men and guns faced each other.

At daybreak Clara watched the beginning through her field glasses, trying to decide where she would be needed most. Presently, far to the right, she saw that the Union forces were being driven back. Cavalry and artillery rushed to support them.

Clara dashed to her wagon. "Follow the cannon," she told her driver.

They followed until the last gun halted on the edge of a corn field, near a house and barn. Some three hundred wounded already lay in the yard, and on the farmhouse porch she could see the surgeons at work. Clara filled her arms with bandages, dressings, and stimulants, and waded through the corn in a deafening roar of artillery. Shells screamed over her head. Bullets whined around her, ripping the corn leaves.

The four surgeons stared at her, dumfounded. Their surgical supplies were already gone, and they had nothing but their instruments and chloroform. They were using green corn leaves to dress the wounds. The long supply train had not yet reached the battlefield.

No one was ever received with greater joy.

All that day Clara and her men worked to feed

and bandage the wounded who must wait their turn with the surgeons. And all that day the battle raged back and forth, first one side winning and then the other. The wounded poured in by the hundreds, covering all the ground around the house and filling the barn. The Union artillery was scarcely a stone's throw away, and blinding, acrid smoke rolled across the farm in billows until Clara could barely see her way as she went from one moaning figure to another.

A soldier caught at her skirt asking for water. As she bent over and lifted his head, a bullet tore through her sleeve and struck the helpless man, killing him instantly. Clara put his head down gently and went on toward the barn.

Just outside the door another wounded man stopped her.

"Please," he said, "what's burning my face so?"

Clara peered at him through the smoke. His face was bulging from a bullet lodged in the cheekbones. When she explained, he implored her to cut it out. This was too much, even for Clara, and she said hurriedly that she would go for a surgeon.

"Oh, no, please!" he begged. "It's only a small wound. I must wait my turn; but the pain is terrible. You can get the ball. *Please!*"

The distressed Clara said miserably, "I can't hurt you so much."

"Lady, you couldn't hurt me any more than this bullet is hurting me now. Please take it out."

Clara took a deep breath, steeled herself, and reached for her pocketknife. Just then a sergeant lying near by, who had been shot through both thighs, pulled himself agonizingly to a sitting position.

"I'll help you with that," he said to Clara.

Inch by inch he dragged himself along the ground, took the other man's head in his hands, and held it tightly while Clara cut out the ball as well as she could and washed and bandaged the face.

"I do not think," she says, "that a surgeon would

have called it a scientific operation, but from the gratitude and relief of the patient I dare to hope that it was successful."

The numbers of fresh wounded were increasing, and late in the afternoon one of Clara's men emerged from the smoke with bad news. The last loaf of bread, the last of the gruel, the last cracker had been used. There were three boxes of wine left. What should they do?

"Open the wine and give that—and God help us," said Clara, and promised herself as of that instant that next time she would bring more wagonloads of supplies.

A moment later she was blessing the women at home who had sent the wine. When the boxes were opened, she found that the bottles had been packed, not in sawdust as usual, but in *cornmeal!* It filled six gigantic kettles with hot cornmeal mush, and Clara was suddenly inspired to examine the farmhouse cellar. She found three barrels of flour and a great bag of salt left by the Confederate Army, which had been there first. It was a gold mine to Clara and her assistants, but it was the cornmeal which made her realize more than ever the value of not bringing anything, even sawdust, unless it could be used.

When darkness came, they unpacked enough lanterns to light the barn, and Clara went to the house.

The head surgeon was sitting alone beside a table on which was burning a fragment of candle. Clara could just see his face in the dim wavering light. He looked ill and desperate.

"You are tired, Doctor," she said.

He stumbled wearily to his feet with the automatic courtesy of those days. "Tired!" he said savagely. "Yes, I'm tired—tired of carelessness, of heartlessness! Here we have at least a thousand wounded men. Five hundred of them cannot live until daylight without attention, and that two inches of candle is all the light we have or can get!"

"Look," said Clara, pointing to the brightly lit barn

"Come here, Doctor." She drew him to the doorway. The brightly lighted barn sent cheerful beams through the battered trees and torn corn. "Look," she said.

He looked without understanding. "What is it?" he asked vaguely.

"Lanterns."

"*Lanterns!* Who did it?"

"I, Doctor."

"Where did you get them?"

"Brought them with me."

"How many have you?"

"All you want—four boxes."

He dashed out without a word and never spoke of the matter again, though the deference he paid Clara was, she says, "almost embarrassing." But he did thank her eventually. Many years later when she was lecturing in a Midwestern city she told this story. When she had finished, a man in the audience sprang to his feet.

"Madam," he said, "I am that doctor. If I did not thank you then, I thank you now."

The Battle of Antietam stopped with the darkness and the guns were quiet, cooling in the moonlight. The armies, victorious Union and defeated Confederate, withdrew. The wounded, the dying, and the dead remained in a deathly stillness all along the eight-mile front. The surgeons, stretcher-bearers, Clara, and her four men worked on.

She stayed at Antietam as long as there was anything left for her to do, or anything with which to do it. Then she jolted the long way back to Washington and went to Assistant Quartermaster-General, Colonel Rucker, who heard with tears her story of the absent supplies.

"Next time, may I have four wagons?" she asked.

He promised, and Clara went home to bed with chills and a fever.

14

The Best Protected Woman

Clara did not remain in bed long. News of fighting in the Shenandoah Valley had her up at once—and off.

Colonel Rucker did not forget his promise of more wagons. This time he furnished Clara with four of them, and with eight or ten teamsters, all civilians, who had been driving for the army for two years. They were tired of war and had sworn never again to drive over the miserable Virginia roads. They were infuriated by Colonel Rucker's order, had never heard of Clara, and resented the idea of being bossed by a woman.

As no one had mentioned this to Clara she was surprised by their behavior.

All the first day on the march the men were surly and obstinate. At four o'clock in the afternoon they decided to camp. Clara said they would go on. They ignored her.

She smiled inwardly and said nothing, but she thought, "More bad boys."

The men unharnessed the mules in an ugly silence. While the animals were being fed and watered, Clara gathered a few fence rails, built a fire, and when the teamsters returned she had a hot and ample supper ready for them.

They ate it heartily, but they could not meet her eyes. Afterward they withdrew and sat together in an uncomfortable clump. At last one of them rose and approached Clara. The others followed at a little distance.

"Miss Barton," the leader began awkwardly, "we—we come to say we're ashamed of ourselves. We ask you to forgive us. We been mean and contrary all day and you treated us like gentlemen. We hadn't no right to expect that supper from you, a better meal than we've had in two years, and you as polite as if we'd been the General and his staff. Will you forgive us? We shan't trouble you no more."

Clara's forgiveness was easy to obtain. She accepted the apology as she would have accepted it from schoolboys, gladly and with understanding. There was a chorus of good nights; then the leader went to Clara's ambulance wagon, where he hung a lantern from the top, spread her quilts, helped her up the steps, and buckled the canvas door tightly. Then he rolled himself in his blankets and lay down close to the wagon steps.

In the morning the teamsters got Clara's breakfast. It was ready when she awoke.

These men were with her for six months, through frost, snow, long marches and battle. They nursed the sick, tended the wounded, sat with the dying, and buried the dead. Their loyalty to Clara grew with the months.

That first day the teamsters were surly and obstinate

She "followed the cannon" through three weeks of fighting in the Shenandoah Valley, returned to Washington for an operation on an infected hand, and went back to the front, once more near Fredericksburg, Virginia, which was now occupied by the Confederates.

She found the Union forces across the river from the town and struggling, under merciless fire, to build a pontoon bridge over the river. From the upstairs windows of houses along the water front, Confederate snipers picked off the Union engineers with deadly accuracy. The crossing was finally made in boats with terrible loss of life. The Union men swarmed into the town, and the Confederates drew back slightly. They still held half the town.

Meanwhile the engineers finished the bridge, and Union reinforcements raced over it almost before it was finished.

The battle was at its worst when the chief surgeon, who had crossed with the troops, sent a courier to Clara. The crumpled, bloody scrap of paper which the man gave her read: "Come to me. Your place is here."

The chief surgeon had evidently not been told that a battlefield is no place for a woman.

Clara's teamsters looked at the pontoon bridge with its hail of fire and turned to Clara with chalk-white faces. "Don't go, Miss Barton! You'll be killed! Send us. We can help him."

Deeply touched, Clara smiled at them. "I *must* go," she said gently, and they knew that argument was useless. So they went with her, staggering across the swaying bridge while the water on both sides hissed with shot. It is doubtful if Clara remembered, at that moment, the unsteady log bridges of her childhood, but her teamsters were astonished at her agility.

When she reached the other side, an officer stepped forward to help her over a pile of lumber at the end of the bridge. As he raised his hands to take hers, a piece of exploded shell screeched between them, slicing off part of her dress and a section of the officer's coat. Clara went on in search of whatever was the hospital. Half an hour later the officer was brought in dead.

As the fighting continued, nearly every house became a hospital. Clara, going from one to another, paused before she crossed the street to let a regiment of Union reinforcements pass. She was seen by an elderly provost marshal who supposed she was one of the women living in the town.

He halted the regiment and galloped up to her. Then, leaning from the saddle, he said kindly, "You are alone and in great danger, Madam. Do you want protection?"

Clara was amused but thanked him warmly. Without explaining who she was, she added with a smile that she believed herself to be the best protected woman in the United States.

The old general was puzzled but the men nearest her in the halted regiment heard and understood, for they all knew her.

"That's right!" they shouted and began to cheer. Rank after rank took it up in a series of crashing roars.

Then the general knew. He removed his hat and bowed. "I believe you are right, Madam," he said and galloped away.

15

Last Years of the War 1863-1865

The Battle of Fredericksburg ended in a truce. In two years of fighting the Army of the Potomac had won a single victory—Antietam. But out West and in Tennessee and Mississippi, General Ulysses Grant had been winning steadily, and the Union Navy had blockaded all the Southern seaports.

After Antietam, President Lincoln issued his famous Proclamation of Emancipation, freeing the slaves in all the rebellious states. With the arrival of the Union troops, many plantations were abandoned. The former slaves flocked into Union camps. So many Negroes left that the plantations were without help of any kind and could produce no crops to feed either the civilian population or the army. Horses, mules, and cattle had been taken by the army. The South was beginning to know real hunger.

It was just now that Clara decided to make a change and work with the armies farther south.

Her reason for this was simply that she wished to be where she would be most needed, and that was where the fighting was heaviest.

She was told that there would not be much more fighting in Virginia, but that the Union intended to capture Charleston and push on, deep into the South. The worst fighting would be there.

There were two other reasons for making this change. David was Quartermaster at Port Royal, South Carolina, and she had a great longing to be with some of her family again. Furthermore, she might be able to find Stephen if she went with the army when it pushed into the interior. Nothing had been heard of him in a year.

So she applied to the War Department for permission to go to Port Royal. The permission was granted at once.

She would have done better to stay with her beloved Army of the Potomac, for she not only missed the terrible Battle of Gettysburg, where she was desperately needed, but she found that army service in Port Royal was not the kind of service for which she had trained herself.

Here were no long marches with her faithful teamsters, no fierce battles where she followed the cannon and worked until she dropped. Instead, she found herself looking on at the siege of Charleston which lasted eight months. She worked in base hospitals and advance hospitals with a great many other women, and there was no occasion to use her particular talents.

There were times when she worked to the point of exhaustion, but there were longer periods when she had little to do beyond giving out a few provisions or nursing the sick. There were plenty of other women who could do that.

She was, however, very happy to be with David and in some ways she had a good time. There were many officers' wives at Port Royal. There were parties and dinners. Clara had her own saddle horse and rode daily, but this was not what she wanted even if she enjoyed it.

To make matters worse, several high-up medical officers became jealous of her. Exactly why is not known. Perhaps too much honor was paid her; perhaps she was too efficient; perhaps the officers were doing something they shouldn't and she knew it.

Whatever the reason, they made things as dif-

ficult for her as they could, commandeering her
tents, waylaying her supplies, whispering about
her. They finally managed to get an order trans-
ferring her to a hospital farther north. She refused to go and went home instead, which did
not endear her to the commanding general.

After a rest at home she went to Washington,
but nobody seemed to need her until the Battle
of Spotsylvania. Once more, it was not far from
Fredericksburg and the wounded were being
taken there. Clara rushed to Colonel Rucker for
passes. He appreciated her and was only too glad
to have her go to the front, for he knew what
she could do.

Happy again, Clara marshaled her wagons and
hurried out of Washington. It was like old times.
She was needed and valued. She was on her own
again, free of petty jealousies, interference and
sly enemies. It was wonderful to be rattling over
the rough roads again, going north to battle.

It was not that Clara loved war. She hated it.

What she loved was service, and nowhere, except in war, had she been able to give enough of herself to satisfy her.

At Fredericksburg landing she came upon two hundred six-mule wagons loaded with wounded who were to be sent by boat to the Washington hospitals. The wagons were stuck hub-deep in soupy mud. As usual, the wounded had had no food or medical care.

This was a situation which Clara could handle automatically. She was looking over the scene deciding where to begin work when a frail young man stepped up to her.

He was a clergyman who, with several others, had been sent to the front by a religious organization known as the Christian Commission. The little group of inexperienced men had come with good hearts, a supply of clothing and little else.

He spoke to Clara timidly, asking if she thought those wagons might contain wounded. She assured him that they did, and that the wounded could not possibly be put on the boats before night—if then.

"Is—could we—do anything for them?"

"Certainly. They must be fed and their wounds dressed."

He was anxious to help but had no idea what to do. Under Clara's direction, he gathered wood and helped build a fire, getting himself well smudged, and looking more fragile than ever.

Clara filled a dozen camp kettles with steaming hot coffee, produced two large squares of cloth which she tied around her waist and that of her wondering helper, pinned up the loose corners to make huge pockets, filled the pockets with crackers, and picked up her kettle. The young clergyman, watching, picked up his, and together they went down the slope to the sea of mud. Here, the unfortunate man halted. In his anxiety to help he had forgotten the mud. He stared at it now, bewildered.

"But how are we to get to the men?" he asked.

"Walk," said Clara briskly and stepped into the icy mud nearly to her waist. He followed her without a word. As Clara said later, "He had taken his first step into military life." She adds that, frail though he seemed, he turned out to be brave and steady under fire, and "stood fearless in the smoke of battle."

Fredericksburg was once more filled with wounded—but with what a difference! The officers in command of the city had no interest whatever in the wounded. Clara overheard one of them saying that it was hard for the refined people of the town to have to open their homes to "dirty, lousy, common soldiers," and he was not going to insist upon it.

The infuriated Clara waited to see if he would keep his word. He kept it. The wounded were left to die in the wagons without care, and she found five hundred half-dead men lying on the cold bloody floor of an old, ramshackle hotel. They were all moaning for water.

The busy surgeons, working always in one place, were totally unaware of the situation.

Clara left her assistants to attend to the men and managed, somehow, to get a light wagon with fast horses. She left for Washington at a gallop, arriving at dusk, went straight to the head of the Senate Military Committee, and told her story. An investigating committee left for Fredericksburg at two o'clock the next morning and arrived at ten. By noon the wounded were being fed from the city's store of food, and the houses were opened to men who had been called the "dirty, lousy, common soldiers" of the Union Army.

After Spotsylvania, she went back to Washington to rest for a month and learned from all sides that the end of the war could not be far off. The ranks of the Confederate Army were greatly reduced and there were no more men to call up. What remained of the army was in rags and living on parched corn, though it fought on, stubbornly and bravely. The civilian population in the South was just as badly off, if not worse. Beef and butter were thirty dollars a pound. Tea was five hundred dollars a pound. Shoes were two hundred. People made shoes of cut-up carpets tacked onto wooden soles. Women lined their dresses with newspapers to keep out the wind.

People in the North had no idea of these conditions. Certainly Clara had not, and she was as well informed as anyone. She was resting in Washington when she was offered the job of Superintendent of the Department of Nurses with the Army of the James. The Union forces were closing in on Richmond.

Clara accepted the offer and went to Point of Rocks in southern Virginia, where she spent a blistering, hard-working summer and part of a cold, rainy winter.

It was here that her brother Stephen was brought to her.

He had been captured by Union soldiers, who refused to believe that he was a Union sympathizer. He was sick when he was captured, was badly treated afterward, and three thousand dollars—all the money he had left of a considerable fortune—was taken from him by two Union officers.

Stephen was dying when he was brought to Clara, but he lingered on, gradually growing worse. Clara nursed him at Point of Rocks through the late fall and early winter and went with him when finally he was sent to a Washington hospital. He died in March, just a month before Richmond was captured.

Six days later the great Confederate general, Robert E. Lee, was forced to surrender his ragged and starving army to General Grant. There were a few more months of fighting in the South, but the war really ended with General Lee's surrender.

Poor Clara, half-sick with grief over Stephen's

death, could only feel a sad relief that the Union was saved. Her personal life was shattered, not only by Stephen's death, but by the end of the war. After four years of unbelievable effort, in which her passion for service had been more than fulfilled, there was suddenly a great vacuum.

What was she to do now?

16

Missing Men

Clara was not left to wonder for long. Since the beginning of her war service, soldiers had been writing to her, very often asking if she had any word of a soldier friend or a brother reported missing. As time went on, the families of soldiers who knew her also wrote, hoping for news of someone missing.

The War Department, at that time, had no definite organization for tracing missing men. Soldiers killed in battle were buried by their comrades who marked the grave if there was anything to mark it with, and who duly reported the deaths to their commanding officers. Great numbers of others were buried in unmarked graves, their deaths unreported; many more simply disappeared and were not heard of again. No one knew whether they were dead, wounded or imprisoned. Their families were frantic.

Clara remembered her own anguish about Stephen and determined to trace as many men as possible, dead or alive.

With this in mind, she went to President Lincoln, who was heartily in favor of the idea. So was the War Department.

President Lincoln wrote a letter which she was to publish in newspapers throughout the country. It urged anyone with information, or inquiries, about missing men to write to Clara

Barton. The War Department gave her a tent and some furniture to be set up in Annapolis, headquarters for the discharge of soldiers. They also gave her some stationery and a small amount of postage.

If this seems not only stingy, but short-sighted, it must be remembered that only Clara had any idea of the tremendous task she was undertaking.

Nothing was said about a salary for Clara, or for the assistants she would most certainly need, or for any other expenses.

President Lincoln would never have permitted this omission. He never knew about it, for he was shot and killed in his box at the theater, by an insane actor. In the resulting confusion and uproar, Clara was forgotten.

Meanwhile the letters were coming in, a hundred a day, and Clara could not handle all this alone. Ten or twelve friends offered their services, including her sister, Sally, but Clara knew that they should be paid. She discussed the matter with Sally who was appalled when Clara announced that she would use her own money to finance the work.

That $10,000 deposited to her account by the desperate young man who had rushed off to the gold fields for her sake, was still in the bank, untouched. With accumulated interest it was now $15,000.

Clara began to draw on it. In six months she had spent over $7,000. At the end of the year all the money was gone, and she was forced to appeal to Congress.

Congress returned her $15,000 immediately, and voted her another $15,000 to continue the work.

The results of Clara's work were beyond all expectation.

She had taken one state at a time, listing all men known to be missing from that state's troops. The list was published with a request for information in the state to which it belonged.

Letters poured in. Soldiers wrote with information about missing comrades. There were letters from missing men who had found their way home. Relatives of soldiers wrote saying that John was out West, or had written from a Southern prison camp saying he was all right.

Little by little, following every clue, Clara eventually located over twenty-two thousand men, living or dead. In addition there were the fourteen thousand graves at Andersonville, Georgia, the site of one of the largest of the Confederate prison camps.

This came about through a young soldier named Dorence Atwater, from Terryville, Connecticut. He had enlisted at eighteen, had been taken prisoner, and was sent to Andersonville.

Because of his clear, precise handwriting—there were no typewriters in those days—he was chosen by the prison commander to keep a record of all prison deaths. The young man knew nothing of the desperate condition of the South. The

Andersonville prisoners ate exactly what the Confederate Army ate—corn. Many were wounded or sick with fevers or dysentery. They died like flies, and young Atwater believed that they were being deliberately starved to death.

He made a second—and secret—list of the deaths, which he kept hidden in the lining of his coat. When he was freed at the end of the war, he brought his list home with him. A minor government official to whom he brought the list brushed the matter aside. There was a great deal of trouble about it later. Meanwhile, Atwater had heard about Clara and brought the list to her. She received it with joy and thanksgiving. There were fourteen thousand names on the list!

Clara, as might be expected, took the list to the right people and the government promptly sent her, with young Atwater and a large working party, to Andersonville, to mark the graves.

It was a difficult and heartbreaking job, but they made a cemetery out of a dreary waste.

Clara still had no salary, and as she worked
for four years, tracing missing men, she had to
earn a living on the side. Encouraged by a friend,
she took up lecturing on her war experiences for
a part of each winter. She covered all of the
Eastern states and most of the Midwest. People
thronged to hear her, and though she never
ceased to be frightened when she came out on

To earn money, Clara lectured on her war experiences

the lecture platform, no one suspected it. She made more money than she had ever made before —and spent a good part of it on her search for missing men.

At the end of four years of this, she found herself, one cold winter's night, in Portland, Maine. The lecture hall was packed. Clara came out on the platform as usual, arranged her notes, smiled at the audience, and opened her mouth. No sound came from it.

Her voice was gone again.

17

Europe 1870-1874

Clara was ill all that winter, but the general public would not give her any rest. Its belief in Clara as a miracle-woman was unbounded. People seemed to think that she could do anything, from arranging an interview with the President for total strangers from Podunk, Iowa, to getting somebody's "Cousin Willie" out of jail.

Mothers wanted government jobs for their sons, wives wanted jobs for their husbands. All sorts of people wanted money. Clara's own relatives, many of them, were no more considerate than the public.

When spring came, she had not recovered either her health or her voice. Her doctor, out of patience, told her that she must go abroad; she could get no rest in this country. She must stay abroad for three years and *do nothing*.

That doctor evidently did not know Clara very well.

She was too worn out to care what she did, and obediently set about packing. But she dreaded sailing alone in her depressed condition and persuaded her sister Sally to go with her.

At this time Clara was forty-seven years old, but in spite of her illness she looked a young thirty.

She and Sally went to Scotland, toured it briefly, and then Sally returned home to her family. Clara went to London and then to Geneva, Switzerland, where she prepared to settle down. Geneva was lovely in summer. Clara had friends there and made others, and for a time she was content.

When cold weather came, however, she was miserable and went to Corsica hoping to warm up. She was not warm, or comfortable, and moved to Switzerland by way of France.

It was the beginning of four years of restless wandering, some startling adventures, and no very marked improvement in health, except for one year—the year of the Franco-Prussian War. She went back and forth, here and there, staying a month in one place, six in another—France, Germany, England, Italy again, Switzerland again, France, England. She met kings, queens and princesses and became a devoted friend of the German Grand Duchess Louise of Baden.

It was during her second summer in Europe that war broke out between France and Germany—the Franco-Prussian War. Clara came to life with a leap when the Grand Duchess Louise asked her to go to Strasbourg to organize war relief work. Later Clara made every effort to get to the front, but this was Europe, and though she received permission to go she had no help in getting there. Her offers to nurse in field hospitals were refused.

At last, with a young Swiss girl, Antoinette Margot, Clara started for the front on her own, thinking that once there she would be allowed to work. When she found the roads blocked, she left her carriage and started to walk. This was a mistake, for neither she nor Antoinette had noticed the blue-black clouds which were rolling across the sky. It was a really severe thunderstorm, almost a cloudburst, and when it struck they were quickly drenched to the skin. A tiny village lay ahead and they ran for it. But they were strangers, there was a war going on, and no one would take them in. An evil-looking woman in a filthy inn finally agreed to let the dripping women spend the night. She hauled them both in through a window into what was obviously a bar, for it was packed with drunken German soldiers.

The soldiers were convinced that these two foreign women were spies. They would have given Clara a very bad time of it if a man, a civilian who spoke English, had not offered to interpret.

While Clara was explaining through the interpreter, a huge and very drunken German corporal strode into the room and noticed Clara. Thinking she was the barmaid, he ordered her to serve him wine. She refused. He repeated the order. She refused again.

With a roar he drew his sword, gave it a twirl, and, pressing the point against her chest, backed her against the wall.

And there they stood, the sword point pricking her flesh through her coat. The smoky, crowded room was suddenly silent.

Clara glanced down at the sword and then up at the man, her penetrating eyes hot with contempt. He held her gaze as long as he could, sheathed his sword with an ugly clash and stamped from the room. Clara had no time to be upset, for her little Swiss friend, Antoinette, had fainted.

After they had gone to bed—a bed of rags crawling with what Clara described as "livestock"—the interpreter who had been so helpful earlier, tried to break into their room through the window. When he saw that both women were awake, he paused and explained that he had come to sleep on the floor in order "to protect" them.

Antoinette, who was too young to know evil when she saw it, was thanking him gratefully, and he had one leg over the sill when Clara sat

The big German corporal backed Clara against the wall

up in bed and said quietly, *"If you come in here, I will kill you."*

The man was not a fool. He withdrew hurriedly.

The next day they gave up all attempts to reach the front or even a hospital. But Clara could not remain idle while a war was going on, and though she eventually saw some of the battlefields it was not until the fighting was long since over.

All that summer and most of the winter, she went from city to city doing relief work, distributing food, clothing and money.

In Strasbourg she founded a "Workroom for Women" where more than three hundred destitute women were given work sewing on cloth bought with funds collected from everywhere and everybody. The clothing they were paid for making was given to homeless refugees.

At this time Clara's health was magnificent.

For her work at Strasbourg the German Emperor gave her a decoration, "The Iron Cross of Merit for Ladies." It was the first of twenty-seven decorations and citations she was to receive before she died.

Chance and Princess Louise put her on the German side. Clara had no interest in who was fighting whom. All she wanted to do was to relieve distress, and she did. Later she did as much in Paris.

At the end of the Franco-Prussian War, Clara's health failed again. Her eyes gave out, and for a time she was half blind.

While she was waiting for her eyes to recover, she received the pleasant news that such money as she had saved from lecturing, and which had been invested, had been increased to such an extent that she was now very well off. She was also tired of Europe and no healthier than when she had arrived there. She tried another long tour of the European countries, but she was homesick now.

When the tour was over, she went home to America, feeling very much at loose ends.

Her years in Europe had been interesting and filled with achievement. She had learned of the existence of an organization known as the International Red Cross. The organization and its work had impressed her greatly. But she was fifty-two, she was tired, she was half sick, and her eyes were in bad shape.

18

A Seed on Good Ground

At the beginning of Clara's stay in Europe, she met a very pleasant and interesting man, Dr. Louis Appia. He was, she learned, a member of the International Committee of the Red Cross. The first time they met he asked her why the United States had not been willing to sign the Treaty of Geneva.

"What," said Clara, "is the Treaty of Geneva?"

"You have never heard of the Red Cross?"

"Only since I was told that you were a member of it."

Dr. Appia smiled. "I would like to visit you again," he said, "and bring you some books about the Red Cross. I will tell you all about it then."

When he returned, Clara listened spellbound to the story of the young Swiss, Henri Dunant, who, while visiting in Italy, had witnessed a terrible and bloody battle between France and Austria, the Battle of Solferino. Dunant had been horrified by the condition of the wounded, who were left lying on the battlefield. He had worked for three days and nights trying to take care of them.

Clara nodded. She understood this only too well.

Henri Dunant had become a banker and a rich man, but he could not forget the wounded soldiers on that battlefield. After thinking and planning for a long time he had a conference with four other influential men, one of them Dr. Appia.

Together they planned an organization which was to be an organization of *nations*. Its purpose was to care for all wounded in time of war, and they drew up an agreement which they hoped would be signed by all civilized nations.

"Why is it called the Red Cross?" Clara wondered.

Dr. Appia called her attention to the Swiss flag, in plain view of her window. It was a white cross on a red field. Dr. Appia reminded her that the organization had been started in Switzerland, by a Swiss.

"We needed an emblem," Dr. Appia said. "Something which could be recognized instantly. Out of honor to Switzerland we simply reversed the flag, making our emblem a red cross on a white field."

"It's beautiful," said Clara, who had always loved red.

The terms of the treaty were simple. Hospitals
flying the Red Cross flag were not to be fired
upon or captured. Surgeons, nurses, chaplains
and attendants were to be considered neutrals
and were to help all alike, taking no sides. People who nursed the wounded in their homes were
to be given military protection.

All nations were invited to attend a meeting
in Geneva and sign the treaty. On August 22,
1864, twelve nations signed. The United States,
England, Sweden and Saxony sent delegates, but
these did not have the power to sign for their
countries. They could only present the treaty to
their governments. Later ten more nations signed
—all, in fact, who had been invited, except the
United States.

The American delegate had been very enthu-
siastic about the treaty, but the United States
had not signed.

"Why?" Dr. Appia asked again.

"I don't know," Clara said.

She did not learn for a very long time after this conversation that the American delegate had taken his copy of the treaty to our Secretary of State, who had stopped it right there. It was a splendid idea, he agreed, but it was concerned only with Europe and with European wars. We wanted no part of either. And that had been the end of that. Neither Congress nor the American people had been told of the treaty.

Clara saw Dr. Appia fairly frequently during her four years in Europe, and each time he spoke to her about the Red Cross. She also had a chance to see it in action during the Franco-Prussian War and had been greatly impressed. The Red Cross had been one of the reasons why she had not been needed on the battlefields.

She discovered that within two weeks of the French declaration of war on Germany the Red Cross Headquarters in Switzerland was ready with supplies, and workers were on their way to the front. Each nation had its own national headquarters. Every town and village had its own Red Cross chapter and a storehouse of supplies.

Clara visited the storehouses in Switzerland and was amazed. "I found there," she says, "a larger supply than I had ever seen at any time in readiness for the field, at our own Sanitary Commission warehouse in Washington."

She noted that all contributions went through at once and were distributed promptly. Wherever a battle occurred, relief was there and ready. Supplies, workers, surgeons and nurses were on hand. The wounded were fed and cared for immediately.

No wonder Clara had not been needed.

She thought of the war at home, the unpreparedness, the long delays in getting supplies to the front. She remembered the surgeon with his lone candle, and the wounded, starving and neglected, at Antietam, Fredericksburg, and Spotsylvania—while the supplies they needed remained in Washington with no means of getting them out.

Clara thought a great deal about the Red Cross. When she sailed for home, Dr. Appia saw her off.

"Will you take up the question of the Red Cross with your government?" he asked.

"Perhaps," said the weary Clara, who had in mind to do so, but who felt, at the moment, that she was incapable of doing anything. Introducing the Red Cross to America would require much thought and planning. Just now she couldn't think.

19

Lone Fighter

It was wonderful to be at home again, to be warm, to be comfortable, to belong; but Clara's happiness did not last for Sally died suddenly. The blow almost killed Clara. One by one her immediate family was going. The only ones left now were David and herself, and David was far from well.

Clara was seriously ill for over a year, so ill
that she could see no one, could not write her
own name. She was nursed back to life, if not
to good health, by Minna Kupfer, another young
Swiss woman like Antoinette Margot, who had
met Clara during the Franco-Prussian War. She
had given Clara German lessons. Clara had nursed
her through pneumonia.

When Minna learned that Clara was danger-
ously ill, she sailed for America at once. She remained with Clara for years, first as nurse and
friend, then as housekeeper. Minna was bright,
cheerful and a good nurse. Somehow she got
Clara on her feet again and taking an interest in
life.

It was not, however, very much of an interest,
and a worried friend urged Clara to try a "water
cure" in a sanitarium in Dansville, New York.
The friend was a sensible woman and Clara,
trusting her judgment, went to Dansville. Here
she found a pleasant atmosphere, good simple

food, and most of all an attitude which suggested that good health is entirely possible. Clara recovered steadily under this cheerful routine and began to enjoy herself. She made so many friends that when she left the sanitarium she bought a lovely old farm on the outskirts of Dansville. It was her home for the next ten years.

Clara had not forgotten about the International Red Cross. She thought about it a great deal, and felt that it lacked something—but what? When she was able, she would try to find out.

She did not feel able for another year, though she kept in touch with Dr. Appia, who had her appointed American representative and gave her much good advice about starting the organization in America. He stressed the point that she should surround herself with a group of interested and capable young people—particularly doctors.

While she was turning all this over in her mind, a young man came to see her. He was

Julian Hubbell, a chemistry teacher in a Dansville school. He had been too young to enlist in the Union Army during the war, but he was not too young to read the newspapers. He had heard a great deal about Clara, her work in the war, and her extraordinary courage. And he had developed a severe case of hero worship.

When he heard that Clara was living right there in Dansville, he called on her at once—and continued to call. Since the Red Cross was on her mind, she spoke about it. Mr. Hubbell was fascinated and begged to be allowed to help.

"What can I do?" he asked.

There was plenty of time, for Clara was not yet entirely well. "Become a doctor," she said, remembering Dr. Appia's advice.

Julian Hubbell not only became a doctor—with only those three words to start him off—but he became Clara's field agent for the Red Cross, and her closest friend as long as she lived.

While he was in medical school at the University of Michigan, Clara went on with her plans. The President, his cabinet, and Congress would have to pass on the Treaty of Geneva. They must be thoroughly informed about it.

She went to Washington for that purpose, talked to everyone she could, and came home discouraged.

No one was interested. She had been shunted from office to office, from official to official, meeting only polite shrugs. Senators and cabinet members made appointments with her and forgot them. Clara was not accustomed to this kind of treatment, but she learned one thing from that first effort. She discovered what was lacking in the International Red Cross.

It was organized only for war and the care of the wounded. There was no provision for peacetime disasters.

Government officials in Washington had made this clear without knowing it. They saw only the word "war," and their immediate response was antagonistic. The United States, they said, was not going to have any more wars, so why go out of its way to get mixed up in European wars. Besides, Europe had done nothing to help the United States during the Civil War. We had to solve our own problems. Let them solve theirs.

Clara said to herself, "The Red Cross here will have to be national before it becomes international, and there must be an amendment to provide for disasters other than war."

With her usual thoroughness she traced back through the years to find out how often we had some great national calamity. She was startled to discover that we had at least one, if not more, every year. We had floods, hurricanes, fires, tidal waves, earthquakes, epidemics and droughts.

These must surely interest the government.

She wrote an amendment to her copy of the treaty, stating that the Red Cross was "to afford assistance to sufferers in time of national or widespread calamities. . . . Organized in every state, the relief societies of the Red Cross would be ready with money, nurses, doctors and supplies to go on call to the instant relief of all who are overwhelmed by any of those sudden calamities which occasionally visit us."

Armed with this and a short pamphlet on the Red Cross which she had written herself, Clara began again.

It was slow, discouraging work, but at last her luck turned. The Civil War veterans of the Union Army had an organization like our present American Legion. It was known as the Grand Army of the Republic, or the "G.A.R." It was politically powerful, and it was all for Clara.

Asked to speak at an enormous G.A.R. convention, she told the men the entire history of the Red Cross in Europe and of her own experience with it. She was talking to men who understood. They were for the Red Cross as one man.

As a result, the Associated Press began to give the subject of the Red Cross some much needed publicity.

President Garfield was much interested, sent for Clara, and promised to bring the matter before Congress. Before he could do so, he was shot by a disappointed office-seeker.

Clara went back to Dansville feeling that she must start all over.

The town of Dansville didn't agree with her. The people were proud of Clara, felt honored that she had chosen their town as her home, and regarded her as their First Citizen.

So the government wouldn't pay any attention to the Red Cross? Very well then, the people of Dansville would. There was no law which forbade their having their own Red Cross.

A delegation went to Clara and asked her to help them organize a local chapter.

Encouraged and delighted, Clara helped them. The local chapter was organized—the first in the

Clara worked at the site of the flood for four months

United States—and had barely collected its first funds and supplies when terrible forest fires broke out in Michigan. Five thousand people were homeless. Unknown numbers had been burned to death.

Clara wired Julian Hubbell, still a medical student at the University of Michigan, and asked him to go to the scene to find out what would be needed and how much. He wired back the information.

Dansville was ready and proud, as well it might have been!

The nearby cities of Rochester and Syracuse rushed to contribute money and supplies, clamoring to have their own Red Cross chapter. Box after box was sent to Michigan and distributed promptly, until the Governor announced that no more were needed.

The entire country was now Red Cross conscious and very much impressed.

Clara rewrote her little book on "The Red

Cross of the Geneva Convention" and offered it for sale. The Associated Press and the New York papers praised it highly, and the book was sold out almost instantly.

Naturally the clamor reached Washington, and the once indifferent Congressmen were indifferent no longer.

At this point, several women, jealous of Clara's prominence, tried to start rival organizations. These flourished long enough to worry and distress Clara, but had no other effect. They died a natural death.

Clara's long fight came to an end at last.

On the first of March, 1882, President Arthur signed the Geneva Treaty and turned it over to the Senate for approval.

While the Senate was deliberating, the Mississippi River overflowed its banks down its entire length causing great loss of life and property.

The infant Red Cross had not had time to accumulate much in the way of funds and supplies. Clara sent out a nation-wide "Appeal to the American People." The newspapers backed her, and the funds poured in. So did food, clothes, medicine, seeds for planting, plows and harrows. Clara forgot nothing. Then, with Dr. Hubbell and a little group of workers, she went to the scene of the disaster and worked there for four months, with such effect that the cities of Memphis, Vicksburg, and New Orleans asked to belong to the Red Cross and have their own local chapters.

Clara had just returned to Washington when the Senate approved the Geneva Treaty and on July 26, 1882, President Arthur issued a proclamation stating that the Government of the United States ratified fully and without challenge its adherence to the Treaty of Geneva. Miss Clara Barton had been appointed president of the National Red Cross.

Clara's real career had begun.

20

A Quarter of a Century

To tell in detail the story of Clara Barton's years of work as president of the Red Cross would require a very long book. Clara, herself, has written that book and called it simply, *The Red Cross*. It has seven hundred pages.

It will be simplest to cover those years with a list, naming places and disasters, but in reading that list one must see behind it a tiny woman, handsome, with beautiful dark eyes and incredible energy.

The words hurricane, fire, flood, war, drought, bring to mind newsreel pictures and the sounds that go with them. Some of us have known these things ourselves; the great trees crashing and the high scream of terrible wind; the dreadful thunder of water gone mad; forest fires choking entire states with smoke; the stinging, blinding sandstorms burying farms and cattle; the people lost, the people found.

Those are the pictures. But Clara is in them —small, lithe, scrambling over debris, sleeping in mud and water, broiling in sun, drenched by rain, strangled by smoke, taking chances in her sixties, in her seventies, in her eighties.

Wherever she went, she brought order, efficiency, sympathy, comfort and, proudly, the banner of the American Red Cross.

Here, then, is the list.

1881   The Michigan forest fires

1882   The Mississippi River floods

1883   The Mississippi River floods

1883   The tornado in Louisiana and Mississippi

1883   The Balkan War

1884   The Ohio and Mississippi floods

1885   The Texas famine

1886   The Charleston earthquake

1888   The tornado at Mt. Vernon, Illinois

1888   The Florida yellow-fever epidemic

1889   The Johnstown flood

1892   The famine in Russia

1893   The tornado at Pomeroy, Iowa

1893 ⎫ The hurricane and tidal wave in the
1894 ⎭   South Carolina Islands

1896   The Armenian massacres in Turkey

1898 ⎫
         ⎬ The Cuban relief
1899 ⎭

1898   The Spanish-American War

1900   The Galveston, Texas, storm and tidal wave

1904   The typhoid epidemic in Butler, Pennsylvania

Clara was doing a few other little things, too. For six months she served as matron of a Massachusetts reformatory for women. She lectured. She wrote books. She bought back part of the old home farm in Oxford, Massachusetts, and spent some part of each summer there. She bought a house in Washington. She went to Europe many times. After the Johnstown flood, where the Red Cross had constructed houses for the homeless, there was lumber left over. Clara sent this to Glen Echo, Maryland, a few miles from Washington, and built a house there to be Red Cross Headquarters. It also became her most permanent home.

In between all these activities, she looked after her various homes, worried about her pets, washed, ironed, cooked, invited all kinds of homeless, or distressed, or sick, or half-crazy people to come and live with her and be looked after.

But even Clara could not go on forever. As she reached her middle eighties, she began to feel tired occasionally. She was still doing work that would have exhausted most women of thirty, but she was surprised to find that after a week or so of constant traveling, speech-making, and hand-shaking, she seemed to need a day or so to be quiet.

Added to this there was trouble in the Red Cross. Several younger women wanted very much to be president, and by this time the organization really had become too big for one person to handle. Clara was more than willing to resign until somebody started rumors to the effect that Miss Barton was getting too old to deal with Red Cross finances, too old to have good judgment, too old to go streaking around the country to floods and hurricanes.

Except for the last, none of these things was true and Clara was hideously hurt. But she was a fighter. She hung on, and she won out, for she was made lifelong president of the Red Cross.

After that she resigned.

But she didn't stop. She was very active in the Women's Relief Corps, she wrote her 700-page history of the Red Cross, she nipped briskly out to Chicago to make a speech, she attended banquets, she visited relatives here and there. She remained gay, charming and gracious.

Nevertheless, the long life was drawing to its end. Clara knew it and did not mind. Her work was done. She would be glad enough to rest.

At ninety she got around to making her will, though she had very little money, now, to leave to anyone. Clara always gave away all her cake.

Once the will was made, she began to let go of life—not in any noticeable way—just a quiet withdrawal. She continued to be interested in everything, from politics and the latest invention to a neighbor's new baby.

That winter she had pneumonia but recovered. The following winter, when she was ninety-one years old, she had pneumonia again, double pneumonia this time. It was the end.

She died at Glen Echo on April 12, 1912. A cousin and Dr. Julian Hubbell were with her.

In those last moments she seemed to be again on the battlefields among the wounded of Antietam, Fredericksburg, Chantilly. She struggled to sit up, throwing off the tender hands which tried to restrain her.

"Let me go!" she cried. "Let me go!"

And she was gone.

Index

179

LANDMARK BOOKS

WORLD LANDMARK BOOKS